A Lion Book
an imprint of
Lion Hudson plc
Mayfield House, 256 Banbury Road,
Oxford OX2 7DH, England
www.lionhudson.com
ISBN-13: 978-0-7459-4874-4
ISBN-10: 0-7459-4874-X

First edition 2003
10 9 8 7 6 5 4 3

Picture acknowledgments

All pictures by Mick Sharp Photography.

Pages 9, 15, 22, 29 © Mick Sharp.
Pages 11, 18, 26, 30, 34, 37, 39, 43, 45 © Jean Williamson/Mick Sharp.

Text acknowledgments

Pages 11, 16a, 16b, 19, 20a, 20b, 23, 27, 28a, 28b, 32, 33a, 33b, 36a, 36b, 37, 38b, 40a, 40b, 41a, 41b, 41c, 44: Scripture quotations taken from the *Holy Bible, New International Version*, copyright © 1973, 1978, 1984 International Bible Society. Used by permission of Zondervan and Hodder & Stoughton Limited. All rights reserved. The 'NIV' and 'New International Version' trademarks are registered in the United States Patent and Trademark Office by International Bible Society. Use of either trademark requires the permission of International Bible Society. UK trademark number 1448790. Pages 13, 17, 24, 38a: Scripture quotations taken from the Authorized Version of the Bible (*The King James Bible*), the rights in which are vested in the Crown, reproduced by permission of the Crown's Patentee, Cambridge University Press. Page 14: Scripture quotation taken from the *New English Bible*, copyright © 1961, 1970 by Oxford University Press and Cambridge University Press. Used by permission. Page 20c: Scripture quotation taken from *The Holy Bible, Living Bible Edition*, copyright © Tyndale House Publishers 1971. All rights reserved. Page 21: Scripture quotation taken from *The Message* by Eugene H. Peterson, copyright © 1993, 1994, 1995, 1996, 2000. Used by permission of NavPress Publishing Group. All rights reserved. Page 24: Introduction inspired by the writings of Mother Teresa of Calcutta and Henri Nouwen. Page 42: 'Expressions of Faith', used by the British Council of Churches' Week of Prayer for Christian Unity in 1988; now widely used as part of Evening Prayer from the Northumbria Community. Page 43: St Columba's Blessing, widely used as part of Evening Prayer from the Northumbria Community.

A catalogue record for this book is available
from the British Library

Typeset in 11.5/14 Calligraphic 421
Printed and bound in Malaysia

The
CELTIC HEART
Reflections for life's journey

Written and compiled
by Liz Babbs

LION

Dedicated to my grandmother Victoria

CONTENTS

When you
make a
journey,
you uncover
a pathway.

Margaret Silf

INTRODUCTION

The Celtic Heart was born out of my own hunger for intimacy with God – that 'something more' that can't be expressed in words. As I travelled around Britain, walking in the footsteps of the Celtic saints, outward journey and ancient pathways inspired inner transformation and kindled within me a desire to help others uncover hidden treasures on their own spiritual journeys.

Whether you are a stranger to prayer, a new pilgrim on the spiritual journey, or an experienced traveller seeking strength and inspiration, this book is for you. And if you're busy, stressed and unable to see the road ahead of you – let alone know where you're going – then *The Celtic Heart* will help you to uncover new pathways, providing sustenance and food for thought. The meditations, images, quotations, prayers, poetry and music offer creative ways to help you connect with God, and can also be used as a springboard for ideas, movements, songs, drawings or times of quiet.

My hope is that each time you read *The Celtic Heart* it will inspire you and draw you closer to the One who guides us on the ultimate journey of discovery.

Liz Babbs

BECOMING STILL There are many ways

of taking 'time out' to become still: silence, music, visual imagery,

reading the Bible... or sitting in the garden or going for a walk.

Your spiritual journey is precious and unique, so there is

no 'right' or 'wrong' way to be with God.

The
unreflected
life is no life
at all.

Sophocles

If your mind is buzzing, write down your thoughts
and distractions, or make a to-do list, and then try again.
You could imagine that God is sitting right next to you like
a trusted friend. Think about what you would like to say to him,
and then spend some time simply enjoying his company. In time,
as you begin to relax into the presence of God, you will become
aware of that still small voice speaking to you and guiding you
in a variety of different ways.

A diary or prayer journal is a useful tool for the journey.
In it you can record your thoughts and feelings, and make a note
of anything you think God might be saying to you. Writing will
help to clarify your thinking and can in itself make you feel less
stressed. Journalling will also help you to deepen your relationship
with God and provide sustenance for the journey. Don't limit
your creativity – be free to draw, stick in pictures or photos,
press flowers, write poetry or prayers. A journal is a personal
and private record of a very intimate dialogue with God that
nobody need ever see, so don't feel restricted. The journals

I have kept over the years charting my own spiritual journey
have become a real treasure. They have also reassured me of
God's loving presence with me, guiding my life and pointing
out landmarks for the next stage of the journey.

Stand at the crossroads and look;
ask for the ancient paths,
ask where the good way is,
and walk in it,
and you will find rest for your souls.

Jeremiah 6:16

ThE JOURNEY

The Celtic heart is very much a journeying heart. The early Celtic missionaries were known as 'people of the coracle', ready to leave the familiar life behind, to embrace creation and to journey wherever the seas might take them.

We find our deepest desire not in our arriving, but in our journeying; not in the finding, but in the searching.

Margaret Silf

We're all on a journey through life, and for many people this is a spiritual journey where we ask questions and seek to discover more about ourselves and God. We're not tourists focused on sightseeing, but pilgrims in search of the Holy, seeking to deepen our relationship with God.

Prayer itself is a journey of discovery into the heart of God. It is not some vague mantra, or a monologue of requests, but a dialogue where we not only speak, but learn how to listen, because God created us to live in a dynamic relationship of communication with him. God doesn't direct us in a 'painting by numbers' way, as that would leave no room for faith or dialogue. And the problems we encounter on the way are our greatest opportunity for exploration and growth.

Thou hast made us for thyself, and our hearts are restless until they find their rest in thee.

St Augustine of Hippo

ThE JOURNEY

The journeys we make express who we are

We journey to be together
We journey to escape
We journey to grow up
We journey to experience
We journey to share
We journey to change things
We journey to be free
We journey to discover
We journey to find ourselves
We journey to come home

But until we find our home in you
our journey is incomplete

Our real journey in life is interior: it is a matter of growth,
deepening, and our ever greater surrender to the creative
action of love and grace in our hearts.

Thomas Merton

Trust in the Lord with all thine heart;
and lean not unto thine own understanding.
In all thy ways acknowledge him,
and he shall direct thy paths.

Proverbs 3:5–6

Happy are those whose refuge is in thee,
whose hearts are set on the pilgrim way!
As they pass through the thirsty valley
they find water from a spring;
and the Lord provides even men who lose their way
with pools to quench their thirst.

Psalm 84:5–6

PEOPLE OF THE WAY

We are People of the Way
searching for landmarks
for our heart's journey

Listening...
to the voice of the spirit

Listening...
to the voice of the soul

Journeying inwards...
towards the pearl of great price

LANDMARKS

To journey...
you must travel

To find...
you must lose yourself

Exploration
risks change

SPIRIT OF CREATION

When we enjoy the beauty and rhythm of the created order, we engage with God, the source of all beauty who spoke creation into being. For God cares about creation like a mother cares for the one to whom she has given birth.

Many of the psalms in the Bible remind us that God speaks to us through the Bible itself and through the wonder of creation. These two 'books' have the potential to reveal God to every person, because we were created for such an awareness.

In the beginning God created the heavens and the earth.

Genesis 1:1

When I consider your heavens,
the work of your fingers,
the moon and the stars,
which you have set in place,
what is man that you are mindful of him,
the son of man that you care for him?

Psalm 8:3–4

The earth is the Lord's,
and the fullness thereof;
the world, and they that dwell therein.
For he hath founded it upon the seas,
and established it upon the floods.

Psalm 24:1–2

A wrong attitude towards nature implies, somewhere,
a wrong attitude towards God.

T.S. Eliot

WATER
PICTURES

Light falls upon bridges
    upon twisted trunks
      that gave up their
        useful life
        long ago
    where swirling leaves
    dance out their days
and light reflected waters
    act as mirrors to the
      soul of creation

The natural world is in many ways a cathedral built with God's own hands. Entering that sanctuary on a warm spring morning, we can easily sense that all of nature joins with us in worship of the Creator. Like the psalmist, we can imagine the trees clapping their hands and the mountains and streams praising God.

RBC Ministries

In the beginning
was the Word,
and the Word was with God,
and the Word was God.
Through him
all things were made;
without him
nothing was made that has been made.
In him was life,
and that life was the light of men.
The light shines in the darkness,
but the darkness
has not understood it.

John 1:1, 3–5

RhYTHMS OF REST

Rest, sleep and recreation are essential to our health and well-being. Rest in particular allows time for reflection and evaluation, as well as an opportunity to discover the next landmark for the journey.

On the journey, rest is not simply inactivity; it enables us to learn how to abide and trust – to let go into the arms of the one who holds our lives in the palm of his hand. The focus is intimacy; learning 'the unforced rhythms of grace'.

Jesus modelled the need for rest, and even the rhythms of nature reflect this need. Land must lie fallow to remain fruitful, and the word 'sabbath' is sometimes used in the Bible to refer to both a year of rest for the land and a day of rest for the people. Many of us, in our busyness, have lost touch with God's natural rhythms and need to retune our lives to restore order and simplicity.

Come with me by yourselves to a quiet place and get some rest.

Mark 6:31

You chart the path ahead of me,
and tell me where to stop and rest.

Psalm 139:3

Are you tired? Worn out? Burned out on religion? Come to me.
Get away with me and you'll recover your life. I'll show you
how to take a real rest. Walk with me and work with me –
watch how I do it. Learn the unforced rhythms of grace. I won't
lay anything heavy or ill-fitting on you. Keep company with
me and you'll learn to live freely and lightly.

Matthew 11:28–30

BALANCE   Lord, I don't know who I am
                                                what I'm doing
        where I'm going any more
                But I give myself to you
                and pray that you can restore

                                        some sense of

                balance and   o
                                    r
                                        d
                                            e
                                                r
            out of this   c h a o s

The best prayer is to rest in the goodness of God, knowing
that that goodness can reach right down to our lowest depths
of need.

Julian of Norwich

This is time apart, a time to be alone with myself and with God. I have given it to myself as gift but also as necessity, because I recognize that this is a priority in my life at this moment. I am coming apart in order that I may find again, and strengthen, that person who I most deeply and truly am before God.

Esther de Waal

There is a time for everything,
and a season for every activity under heaven:

a time to be born and a time to die,
a time to plant and a time to uproot,
a time to kill and a time to heal,
a time to tear down and a time to build,
a time to weep and a time to laugh,
a time to mourn and a time to dance,
a time to scatter stones and a time to gather them,
a time to embrace and a time to refrain,
a time to search and a time to give up,
a time to keep and a time to throw away,
a time to tear and a time to mend,
a time to be silent and a time to speak,
a time to love and a time to hate,
a time for war and a time for peace.

Ecclesiastes 3:1–8

In quietness and in confidence shall be your strength.

Isaiah 30:15

SEEDS OF SILENCE

In order to find the pathway that leads to intimacy with God, we need to rediscover the gift of silence, for it is in the silence of the heart that God speaks. In the silence we learn how to shed the baggage that so easily clutters our lives and the noise that can be like spiritual pollution.

Silence is the language of lovers, enabling us to draw closer to the Father-heart of God. It is as we engage with the mystery of silence that we realize that our temporary withdrawal helps us to be more fully present with others.

It is silence and stillness that, in my experience, people most want to learn and deepen.

Martin Shaw

Silence is the discipline that helps us go beyond the entertainment quality of our lives. There we can let our sorrows and joys emerge from their hidden place and look us in the face, saying: 'Don't be afraid; you can look at your own journey, its dark and light sides, and discover your way to freedom.'

Henri Nouwen

God is a friend of silence. His language is to 'Be still, and know that I am God' (Psalm 46:10). He requires us to be silent to discover him. In the silence of the heart God speaks.

Eileen and Kathleen Egan

Silence is making friends with time. It does not fight it or waste it, it refuses to run after it. Silence floats free with time, letting the pattern of the moments unfold at its own pace. In silence we break the hold time has on us, and accept in practice that our true home is in eternity.

Sister Wendy Beckett

TIME

We live upon its

k
  n
   i
    f
     e
    e
  d
  g
   e

We do not own time
Time moves
in
relation to God

OASIS OF PEACE

> We have an absolute need for quiet, for the heart's wordless resting on God.
>
> Sister Wendy Beckett

The busyness of our lives can lead us to a place of spiritual and emotional bankruptcy. But God not only promises to shoulder our anxieties, but to give us the gift of his peace and rest. A divine exchange takes place where we can give our problems to God, for he promises to carry them for us so that we can walk free.

Peace is also about trust – learning how to surrender ourselves into the arms of our Creator Father, who invites us to relax and enjoy his company.

Be still, and know that I am God.

Psalm 46:10

WATERSCAPE

Water
  stills my soul
    calms my
      mind
        brings peace
          to
            my
              inner
                being

27

'And in this place I will grant peace,' declares the Lord Almighty.

Haggai 2:9

The places we count sacred touch us on a number of levels: sometimes their beauty delights the eye, often we can sense God's presence or the prayers of others, always there is a story that touches heart and mind.

From the Northumbria Community

SECRET
STONES

Cold angularity
warms my hands
breathes
new life

The hidden colours
of turquoise
draw me
to secret places
with so many stories to tell

Peace I leave with you;
my peace I give you.
I do not give to you as the world gives.
Do not let your hearts be troubled
and do not be afraid.

John 14:27

PEACE PRESENCE

The calm of a summer night
embodies the peace of God

The beauty of a sunset
embodies the truth of God

The glory of the dawn
embodies the faithfulness of God

Everything in all creation
shouts the reality of God

LIGHT OF THE WORLD

Light of the world
infiltrate my darkness

Light of the world
restore my strength

Light of the world
illuminate my pathway

and grant me your peace
that I might find my way
home to you

CORDS OF LOVE Learning to receive

I will
instruct you
and teach you
in the way
you should go.

Psalm 32:8

God's love is essential for our physical, mental and emotional health.

For it is only as we allow our roots to go down deeper into the rich

soil of God's love that we will gain the life-giving nourishment

needed to sustain us on our spiritual journey.

As we learn to accept ourselves as beloved children
treasured by a loving parent, then we are free to
venture along any pathway and to enjoy the adventures
along the way. For God is both our companion and our guide,
pointing out the landmarks.

THANKSGIVING

Thank you, Lord,
for the cutting and weaving
for that first umbilical knot
you were shaping
and forming
all that I was to become

Thank you, Lord,
for the 'ups' and 'downs'
the 'unders' and the 'overs'
you were weaving
beauty and purpose
into my life

How great is the love the Father has lavished on us,
that we should be called children of God!

1 John 3:1

For you created my inmost being;
you knit me together
in my mother's womb.
I praise you because I am
fearfully and wonderfully made;
your works are wonderful,
I know that full well.
My frame was not hidden from you
when I was made in the secret place.
When I was woven together
in the depths of the earth,
your eyes saw my unformed body.
All the days ordained for me
were written in your book
before one of them came to be.

How precious to me are your thoughts, O God!
How vast is the sum of them!
Were I to count them,
they would outnumber the grains of sand.
When I awake,
I am still with you.

Psalm 139:13–18

Love is the response of the heart to the overwhelming
goodness of God.

Richard Foster

PRECIOUS
STONES

We hold each other's lives
in our hands
What fragility and responsibility
Earthen vessels formed
from loving hands
So easily crushed
by clumsy words and actions
and only forgiveness can reassemble the parts
according to the Maker's instructions

TOUCHSTONES

Lord of all life
grant us forgiveness
for our judgmental thoughts
and wrong attitudes
for the poverty of our actions
and the words
with which we
wound

DANCE OF JOY

I have come that they may have life, and have it to the full.

John 10:10

God wants us to enjoy the whole of our journey through life. It's not an endurance test – though sometimes it might seem like it! In the Old Testament, God instructed his people to eat, sing, dance and celebrate. Jesus' first miracle was to make wine for a party.

There are some people who radiate such natural joy that you cannot fail to be moved by it. For their joy reminds us that we are blessed at every turn.

To express joy is to be alive to that childlike quality within, where hope dances freely across the face of adversity. It's only as we learn how to celebrate all aspects of our life that we can fully understand the true meaning of joy. For the joy of the Lord is our strength.

You will go out in joy
and be led forth in peace;
the mountains and hills
will burst into song before you,
and all the trees of the field
will clap their hands.

Isaiah 55:12

The meadows are covered with flocks
and the valleys are mantled with corn;
they shout for joy and sing.

Psalm 65:13

The glory of God is a human being fully alive. It is in the
awesome sunshine of God's presence that true joy abounds.

St Irenaeus of Lyon

LORD OF
CREATION

Open my eyes
to your glory
Release my heart
to dance

THREEFOLD JOY

Joy of the Creator Father
Joy of the Redeeming Son
Joy of the Sustaining Spirit
Joy of the Three in One

Thou wilt show me the path of life:
in thy presence is fullness of joy;
at thy right hand there are pleasures for evermore.

Psalm 16:11

LIVING WATER

Streams of living water
burst forth with fountains of joy
and I am soaked –
soaked in the river
of your love

Deep calls to deep
in the roar of your waterfalls;
all your waves and breakers
have swept over me.

Psalm 42:7

Now we see but a poor reflection as in a mirror; then we shall see face to face.

1 Corinthians 13:12

THE JOURNEY BEYOND Life is a

journey that passes through many different seasons. Death may be

the end of our physical earthly journey, but it is not the end of our

spiritual journey. 'The dust returns to the ground it came from,

and the spirit returns to God who gave it' (Ecclesiastes 12:7).

For those who have a relationship with God, death is a doorway to new life. It is not a full stop, but a hyphen that links us to the eternal presence and love of God. Death is like going backstage to meet the author of every word ever written across creation.

AT THE VORTEX

It's at the vortex of light and dark
  pain and suffering
    hopelessness
    and despair
      that I
      find
        y
        o
        u

40

We all lose as we walk through life,
but grief is a friend, not a foe,
a teacher of wisdom,
a creative experience that draws us closer to God.

When all falls apart in despair and sadness,
in God we are sustained
because he has been there before us
and grieves with us.

Who is to measure the length of a life except God?

But we are enriched through the lives of others
and are carried on the wings of their prayers,
and our friends sent like missionaries from the heart of God
speak words of comfort to our fears.

Your word is a lamp to my feet and a light for my path.

Psalm 119:105

I am the way and the truth and the life.

John 14:6

I am the resurrection and the life. He who believes in me
will live, even though he dies; and whoever lives and believes
in me will never die.

John 11:25–26

Lord, you have always given
bread for the coming day;
and though I am poor,
today I believe.

Lord, you have always given
strength for the coming day;
and though I am weak,
today I believe.

Lord, you have always given
peace for the coming day;
and though of anxious heart,
today I believe.

Lord, you have always kept
me safe in trials;
and now, tried as I am,
today I believe.

Lord, you have always marked
the road for the coming day;
and though it may be hidden,
today I believe.

Lord, you have always lightened
this darkness of mine;
and though the night is here,
today I believe.

Lord, you have always spoken
when time was ripe;
and though you be silent now,
today I believe.

From the Northumbria Community

See that ye be at peace among yourselves, my children,
and love one another.
Follow the example of good men of old,
and God will comfort you and help you,
both in this world
and the world which is to come.

St Columba's Blessing

And so, Lord,
somewhere in the distance we meet
Is it eternity
or some future time
Is there a nowness about it
a separation
and beyond
an otherness
but
togetherness
walking hand in hand
across
the
sands
of
time

And surely I am with you always,
to the very end of the age.

Matthew 28:20

Track Titles

Becoming Still

The Journey

Spirit of Creation

Rhythms of Rest

Seeds of Silence

Oasis of Peace

Cords of Love

Dance of Joy

The Journey Beyond

You can contact the author on liz@lizbabbs.com or visit her website www.lizbabbs.com